Stylish
DECOUPAGE

Stylish
DECOUPAGE

15 step-by-step projects to dazzle and delight

MARY MAGUIRE

LAUREL
GLEN

San Diego, California

Laurel Glen Publishing
An imprint of the Advantage Publishers Group
5880 Oberlin Drive, San Diego, CA 92121-4794
www.laurelglenbooks.com

All notations of errors or omissions should be addressed to Laurel Glen Publishing, Editorial Department, at the above address. All other correspondence (author inquiries, permissions, and rights) concerning the content of this book should be addressed to New Holland, Garfield House, 86 Edgware Rd, London, W2 2EA, England.

Library of Congress Cataloging-in-Publication Data

Maguire, Mary.
      Stylish découpage : 15 step-by-step projects to dazzle and delight / Mary Maguire.
         p. cm.
      Includes index.
      ISBN 1-59223-230-2
         1. Decoupage. I. Title: Découpage. II. Title.

   TT870.M233 2004
   745.54'6--dc22

                                        2003065881

1 2 3 4 5 08 07 06 05 04

Senior Editor: Clare Hubbard
Editor: Anna Southgate
Production: Hazel Kirkman
Design: AG&G Books; Glyn Bridgewater and Jane Skinner
Photography: Shona Wood
Editorial Direction: Rosemary Wilkinson

Reproduction by Pica Digital Pte Ltd, Singapore
Printed and bound in Malaysia by Times Offset (M) Sdn. Bhd.

DISCLAIMER
The author and publishers have made every effort to ensure that all instructions given in this book are safe and accurate, but they cannot accept liability for any resulting injury or loss or damage to either property or person, whether direct or consequential and howsoever arising.

CONTENTS

Introduction *6*

Materials *8*

Equipment *10*

Paints, Pastes, and Varnishes *12*

Painting and Preparation *14*

Preparing the Images *16*

Composition *18*

Pasting an Image *19*

Napkin Technique *20*

Using Foils *21*

Varnishing *22*

Troubleshooting *23*

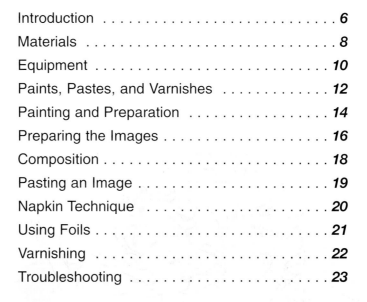

PROJECTS

Featherweight Lampshade *24*

Sweet Cherry Coat Hangers *27*

Patchwork Frame *30*

Letter Rack *33*

Scrumptious Platter *36*

Seashore Drawers *39*

Magazine Rack *42*

Easter Eggs *45*

Polka Dot Tray *48*

Fairy Box *52*

Sky Screen *56*

Fireplace Screen *60*

Chintz Chairs *64*

Jewelry Box *68*

Christmas Box *72*

Templates *76*

Suppliers *78*

Index *80*

INTRODUCTION

Découpage is one of the easiest crafts to master, and although it is basically cut and paste, it can be elevated to a fine art through practice, skill, and creativity, just like any other craft.

Traditionally, découpage was finished with up to twenty layers of varnish. Each layer would have been sanded before the next was applied, so that a smooth, glossy, lacquerlike finish was achieved. There would be no irregularities on the surface and the pasted-on print

Right: **This screen has been decorated with shapes cut from origami paper (see page 59).**

could be passed off as a painting. The practice originated in Italy, where it was called *lucca contraffatta* (imitation lacquer). The Italians discovered that hand coloring prints and pasting them onto furniture helped satisfy the demand for the considerably more expensive hand-painted works of great artists. They perfected the technique until it became an art form. Its popularity spread throughout Europe, and it became a common pastime for ladies, even

nobility: Marie Antoinette is said to have been fond of cutting up her oil paintings and pasting them onto furniture. In fact, the word "découpage" is French.

The craft reached the height of its popularity during the Victorian era, when cheap, mass-produced printed images became available to a wider market. It was so popular that partially cutout images were manufactured specifically for découpage. Many of the designs are still being produced today and some of them appear in this book.

This book offers a series of projects for both novice and advanced découpage artists. Many of them use medium density fiberboard (MDF) blanks, which are made for decorating and are available in craft and hobby stores. The same techniques can also be applied to old or secondhand items, provided that all the necessary preparation is carried out beforehand. The advantage of MDF is that it has a

Above: **In addition to the MDF blanks available at craft stores, there is a wide range of objects that make ideal surfaces for découpage. Small sets of wooden drawers are inexpensive, nicely proportioned and very useful. Shoe boxes are easy to get ahold of and make very nice gifts, once decorated. Scour thrift stores to find unusual items such as lampshades and crockery.**

smooth finish, no grain, and is stable. For the most part, the projects in this book move away from the old, antiqued look often associated with découpage in favor of a brighter, breezier approach, using a wide range of fresh pastel-colored paints and floral imagery. Today, most of us are happy to use découpage purely decoratively. We don't want to pretend it is painted on, so the laborious process of applying twenty coats of varnish is not necessary, as long as you make sure you apply enough coats to protect your prints from wear and tear.

Choosing, cutting, and creating designs is a fun and relaxing way to spend your time. All sorts of objects can be used as a base, either as an embellishment for your own home or as a gift for someone. Interesting images can be found in magazines and old books, on seed packets, paper napkins, letters, maps, and wrapping paper. You can use copyright-free source books, CDs, or Victorian scraps. There is plenty to choose from. Do respect the copyright laws, however, which are there to protect originators from having their images exploited. Most publishers will be happy to give you permission provided you are not manufacturing items for sale.

MATERIALS

You can use wallpaper, old book illustrations, letters, musical manuscripts, postcards—

the list goes on. If you are reluctant to use originals, scan or color copy them.

1. Wallpaper: Look through wallpaper books to find interesting and funky designs. Ask your local supplier to keep old sample books for you.

2. Wrapping paper: This is probably the most accessible and widely used source material for découpage. It is the right thickness and is available in an abundance of designs.

3. Paper napkins: These have recently become very popular for découpage, and the range of designs is now far greater than ever before. They often have a festive theme, so collect them when you see them as stocks will change to suit the season.

4. Découpage papers: Some craft stores stock papers specially designed for découpage. Designs include musical manuscripts, antique handwriting, and images of fishes and birds.

5. Color copies and printouts: If you don't want to use an original image, you can take it to your local copy store, where they will color copy it for you (although this can be expensive). Alternatively, if you have a good scanner and printer, you can do it yourself. Experiment with different kinds of paper to find out which are the best to use. Fabric,

feathers, and leaves can also be scanned or copied, but be careful not to scratch the surface of the scanner or copier.

6. Stickers: These can also be used in découpage, as long as they can be varnished over. Test them first.

7. Victorian scraps: There is a wide variety still being produced today (see pages 78–79 for suppliers). These charming embossed images are already partially cut out, which makes them very easy to use .

8. Foils: Keep your candy wrappers! Smoothed out, they will make a great source material for your designs.

9. Copyright-free source books and CDs: Books and CDs containing copyright-free images are available on all sorts of subjects, including Christmas, animals etc. (see pages 78–79 for details).

10. Origami papers: These small, square sheets of paper tend to have miniature patterns, making them ideal for découpage; see the variation of the Sky Screen on page 59.

STORAGE
It is useful to be able to store any unused cutout for a later date. Plastic-covered pages from a photo album are ideal for this purpose. They will hold the shapes flat and protect them from dust and damage.

EQUIPMENT

You don't need a lot of equipment for découpage, but if you are intending to do a lot of

it, invest in good-quality brushes, scissors, a cutting mat, and a craft knife.

Note: When using any equipment, you should always follow the manufacturer's instructions.

1. Muslin: This fine, open-weave, cotton cloth is ideal for wiping newly sanded surfaces.

2. Brushes: Iinvest in good-quality brushes if you intend to make a hobby of this craft; they won't shed hairs.

3. Roller/brayer: This is useful for flattening down your pasted design and getting rid of any trapped air bubbles.

4. Sponge: You will need a clean, soft sponge for wiping over a freshly pasted design to remove any surplus paste.

5. Fine brushes: Good-quality, fine-headed brushes with broad, flat, blunt ends are especially useful.

6. Plastic wrap: This is handy for covering surfaces in order to protect them from paint, but also for covering pots of paint and paste mixtures to prevent them from drying out as you work.

7. Face mask: Wear one of these for protection against sanding dust, stray powder particles, and fumes when you spray varnish.

8. Sponge spreaders: These are useful for spreading paste. Beneath the sponge head, there is a firm plastic core that gives the tool more body.

9. Knife: It is good to have a slim, blunt-ended knife for peeling off unsatisfactory prints.

10. Plastic wallets: These are very useful for storing images.

11. Protractor, pencil, and ruler: You will need these for planning out your designs. Choose a hard pencil and make sure the point is sharp.

12. Reusable putty: This is invaluable for positioning images. It enables you to tack elements of your design into place so that you can look at them from a distance.

13. Craft Knife: A craft knife is important for cutting out tiny interior areas that are difficult to reach using scissors. Make sure you always use a sharp blade, as blunt ones tend to tear or buckle the paper.

14. Cutting mat: If you do craft work often, you will find a cutting mat useful. Otherwise, improvise with a piece of cardboard, linoleum, or a thick wad of newspaper.

15. Scissors: You will need a pair of scissors with fine, sharp points.

Embroidery scissors are good for cutting out fine detail. You will also need a large pair of paper or general-purpose scissors for cutting out larger areas. Keep both of these specially dedicated to découpage.

16. Spatula: Use to smooth out freshly pasted prints and to get rid of any trapped air bubbles.

17. Decorators' and masking tape: Decorators' tape is a smooth-surfaced low-tack tape, while masking tape has a slightly crinkled surface. They are both used to mask out areas for painting and for achieving straight lines.

18. Lining paper: Be sure to have a large supply of lining paper, scrap, or newspaper before you start a project. A new sheet for each pasting is the best way to avoid mishaps.

19. Lazy Susan: A lazy Susan is a round wooden board that revolves on a smaller base. It is very useful for doing craft work, as you can turn your artwork without needing to touch it. A lazy Susan is particularly useful for varnishing—just be sure to cover it with plastic wrap or foil before you start.

20. Mixing bowl: Use old bowls for mixing paint and paste. Plastic ones are good and easy to clean.

21. Cloths: Keep a pile of old cotton cloths around as you are working so that you can mop up spills and wipe paintbrushes with minimum effort.

22. Manicure scissors: These are good for cutting out fine detail. They often have curved edges, which can be ideal. Keep them solely for this purpose!

23. Tweezer scissors: The squeezing action of these very

sharp, tweezerlike scissors, ensures a fine, smooth cut. They are available with both straight and curved points (see pages 78–79 for suppliers).

24. Cotton swabs: These are very useful for dabbing away little pockets of glue that collect in awkward places.

25. Cocktail sticks and pins: These can be useful for applying tiny amounts of glue.

26. Dollmaker's needle: This needle is long and straight enough to go through an egg, while the eye is big enough to thread thin ribbon through.

27. Sandpaper: Available at hardware and home improvement stores, it comes in a range of gauges from coarse to very fine. For sanding between layers of paint, use a very fine paper; for stripping off old paint, use a coarse paper.

PAINTS, PASTES, AND VARNISHES

Many different kinds of paint can be used for découpage. I've chosen to use emulsions as they come in a wide range of colors and can be bought inexpensively in small tester sizes.

Note: When using any product, you should always follow the manufacturer's instructions.

1. Spray varnish: Although this is more expensive than conventional varnish, it is quicker to apply and the drying time is very fast. It is available in matte, gloss, and satin finishes. The projects in this book were made using either Plaka matte varnish or a triple gloss varnish.

2. Decorators' varnish: This product has been devised specially for fine decorative finishes. It is a thin, milky, water-based liquid, available in a flat, satin, and gloss finishes.

3. Tissue paste: This is a light paste, manufactured solely for use with napkins.

4. High-gloss varnish: Most of the projects were created using water-based paints and varnishes. For a really glossy finish a varnish devised for polymer clay is recommended.

5. Wallpaper paste: Although useful for projects made with wallpaper, this is also good for making up your own découpage paste mix (see page 19 for details).

6. White school glue: This general-purpose glue can be used alone on heavier papers or mixed with wallpaper paste for use on lighter papers.

7. Sticks: These are extremely useful for mixing paints and paste. Make sure they are smooth and will not shed bits of bark into your paint.

8. Bronze powders: These are extremely fine metallic powders, which can be mixed with a special medium, glue, or varnish to give a metallic finish or luster to a piece. They are available in a large range of colors including purple, green, and blue.

9. Three-dimensional paints: These squeezable bottles of paint come complete with nozzle lids that enable you to pipe out decoration. The paint stays raised once dry—like icing—and gives an embossed effect to your work. They are available in a range of colors and finishes, including metallic, pearl, and sparkle. They are available from craft stores.

10. Acrylic paint: These small pots of paint can be used to paint eggs. They come in a range of pretty, pale pastel colors.

11. Primers: Use white primer for projects with light finishes and gray for darker ones. I have used water-based primers, which are suitable to go under emulsion paints and are easier to wash out of brushes.

12. Felt-tip pens: If you want to add a bit more color to your prints, to color in black and white prints, or to make the white edges of cutouts disappear, you can use felt-tip pens. You can get these in subtle colors from good art-supply stores. Before using them, test them out with paste and varnish to make sure the colors don't bleed.

13. Emulsion paints: Available in a much wider selection of colors than oil-based paints, these have the added advantage of being available in small tester pots. These water-based paints are relatively quick-drying. They are easy to use but must be protected using a varnish.

PAINTING AND PREPARATION

It is worth spending time on preparation. The finished product will look better and last

longer, but it does require practice and patience.

Whether you are using a new MDF board or an old wooden or painted object, all of the surfaces must be sanded smooth: Varnish magnifies any imperfections in the paintwork. Even with MDF board, there are often gaps where the surfaces haven't quite joined smoothly. These can be filled using decorators' filler. If you are decorating older or antique items, you might find wormholes or scratches. You may wish to keep these to add character to the piece, but if not, they can be filled using wood filler.

SANDING

Sandpapers come in various grades and, depending on your surface, you will need to select accordingly. For most of the MDF items in this book, I have used a silicone carbide 400-grit paper. If you are working on wood or previously painted surfaces, you will probably need coarser paper. Ask your local hardware store for advice. It helps to wrap your sandpaper around a small block of

wood, as this will give you a better grip. If your fittings (hinges or catches) are on the surface and visible, you may want to remove them until the painting is complete. An alternative option is to cover them with masking tape to protect them. Always wear a face mask when sanding.

PRIMING

Priming seals the surface of an object prior to painting. For all of the projects in this book, I have used a water-based primer—white for light finishes and gray for dark. Before you start priming, remove the surface dust with a muslin cloth, then paint the surface with a smooth, even layer of primer. When working on wood, always brush in the direction of the grain.

PAINTING

When painting an object with recesses, it is always best to start from the inside and paint outward. Before you start, stir the paint

gently to make sure it is mixed thoroughly. Do not shake the can, as this will create air bubbles. For the majority of projects in this book I have used emulsion paint, which is then sealed with varnish. You will need a broad, flat brush to spread the paint evenly over the surface.

SANDING PAINTWORK

Once the paint has dried thoroughly, it will need a light sanding. This will smooth out any irregularities and get rid of the more obvious brush marks. Rub a dry, soft muslin cloth over the surface to clean up any paint dust before applying a second coat of paint. Always wear a face mask when sanding.

BRONZE POWDERS

MASKING

To mask out a specific area—as for a border—use low-tack decorators' tape. If you need to mask a curve, cut slots along one edge of the tape at ½ in. intervals, and ease the tape around the curve.

EMBOSSING

These are fine metallic powders, and are available in a surprising range of colors, in addition to the obvious gold, silver, or bronze. They can be mixed with a special medium or, alternatively, with glue or varnish. The trick is to get an even suspension of powder in the liquid so that the particles are well distributed once painted (see photograph above). These powder particles are very fine and you should wear a face mask when using them. Try to avoid disturbing the powder.

Paint the metallic mix on smoothly. Try not to overlap areas, as you will get a denser distribution of powder (see photo below).

Use a three-dimensional paint to embellish a design. The paint tube has a long nozzle that acts like an icing bag. Regularly check that the nozzle isn't blocked with dried paint. If it is, you can usually dislodge it by using a pin. Leave plenty of drying time after applying three-dimensional paint.

PREPARING THE IMAGES

Before you start, it is essential that you have a good pair of sharp scissors. Furthermore,

any paper that isn't colorfast will need to be sprayed first with a fixative or varnish.

This will ensure that the colors don't bleed during the gluing or varnishing stages. Hold the can 8 in. away from the paper and spray evenly over the surface. A great trick is to spray very lightweight papers, which makes them more robust for cutting and pasting.

ISOLATING IMAGERY
When cutting an image from a busy pattern, it helps to isolate it first by drawing around it.

CUTTING OUT INTERIOR AREAS
Small, detailed areas are best cut out before the whole isolated image is cut from a sheet of paper. This will give you greater stability and reduces the risk of tearing. Use a self-healing mat and a craft knife. Check that the blade is sharp—a blunt blade will tear the paper. (See photo above right.)

GENERAL CUTTING
Cut out an isolated image using a medium-to-large pair of scissors. Take care not to cut across any image you might want to use later (see photo right).

CUTTING EDGES
You will need to use a small pair of scissors for cutting the final outlined edges of an isolated image. Manicure scissors are good for this. Practice on magazine images. Cut around your shape, directing the scissors from beneath the paper so that only the points are visible. This will make it easier for you to see where you are cutting. Hold the scissors with a relaxed hand, tilted upward (gives the edge of the paper a slight bevel). Guide the paper into the blades, reserving the tips for intricate edges. Every so often, cut off surplus paper and discard. (See photo right.)

CUTTING CURVES TO FIT OBJECTS

There are two ways of doing this. The first is by placing your object on top of the print in the desired position, and tracing along the curve with a pencil. This can then be cut. The second method, shown here, is to tack the image into position, use your finger to rub along the edge of your object—its shape will be embossed onto the paper—and then you can cut it out.

INTERLOCKING IMAGES

If your final composition involves several different shapes that touch each other, you may want to make sure that the images line up neatly without gaps instead of merely overlapping. This can be done quite simply by cutting an excess amount at the end of each shape at the

point at which it should meet another. Line two such shapes up on the cutting surface, each with a slight overlap. Stabilize them with tiny bits of reusable putty, and cut through both overlapping prints along the line you want to join.

Make sure your blade is sharp and that you cut through both prints completely. You will need to press down firmly to secure the prints and prevent any movement.

THICKENING FINE LINES

This is a useful tip for helping to cut out fine lines. Before cutting, choose a crayon or felt-tip pen (make sure it is colorfast) the same color as the image to be cut out and color around fine lines to thicken them up. (See photo below.)

LOSING WHITE EDGES

If your cutout images are dark and they are going to be stuck onto dark backgrounds, the white edges of the paper will show up. To get rid of these white edges, use a color felt-tip pen or crayon that matches either the print or the background. Check first for colorfast compatibility with your varnish.

COMPOSITION

Beauty is in the eye of the beholder and only you can decide what composition will please

you. Spend time shuffling your prints around until you achieve an appealing arrangement.

Don't rush this process—it's better to spend time getting it right at this stage rather than having to peel off an unsatisfactory design later on.

BACKGROUND

For a design with many different elements, first decide what is going to be used as the background. This will tend to be the largest of your cutouts. Tack down this image first, using reusable putty.

CREATING A RHYTHM

Build up the design with smaller elements. Here, smaller blossoms have been added to give the design a circular or wreathlike quality.

FOREGROUND ELEMENTS

Start to place the elements in the foreground, tacking them in place with reusable putty as you go. Be careful not to overwhelm the background. Generally, more detailed images will be in the foreground. (See photo right.)

MARKING POSITIONS

Using a sharp pencil, lift the edges of the tacked prints slightly away from the surface so that you can mark their positions with a dotted line—just to the inside of where the edge will lie—so once pasted, the marks will not show.

PASTING AN IMAGE

Once you are certain of a composition and have it clearly marked out on your object,

you can begin to paste the prints into position.

Always use a new sheet of newspaper for each pasting. The thickness of the glue you use will depend on what type of paper you are gluing—a heavier, thicker paper will require a thicker paste, while tissue paper needs a thinner mix. Many of the découpage glues on the market have a PVA base.

MIX A PASTE

Following the manufacturer's instructions, mix up some wallpaper paste in a jar or pot with a fitted lid (you will probably only need to use a fraction of the packet depending on how much découpage you are doing). Once this is mixed, add roughly an equal quantity of glue and mix thoroughly until the two are completely blended. The wallpaper paste will give the resulting mix a more slimy texture; this allows more leeway when positioning the prints, as white school glue tends to adhere too quickly.

APPLYING THE PASTE

Lay the print, image-side down, on a sheet of scrap paper and spread the glue evenly, making sure that it reaches all edges. Don't worry if you go over the edges, but don't move your print as the paste may get onto the front of the image and pull off the surface color. Set the print into position. Smooth it out from the center with your fingers. Use a spatula to help spread the image and to force out any excess glue. Be careful not to press too heavily, or you may scrape off the surface of your print. (See photo above.)

REMOVING EXCESS GLUE

Remove excess glue by wiping over your object with a barely damp sponge. Repeat until all the surface glue has been removed. (See photo above right.)

TRAPPED GLUE

Any paste trapped in "cutaway islands" can be removed with the tip of a cotton swab.

NAPKIN TECHNIQUE

This easy technique is becoming more and more popular. The source material is paper napkins,

which are now available in a vast range of pretty and varied designs.

Only the surface layer of the tissue is used—it is very fine, which makes it ideal for découpage.

SEPARATING THE TISSUE

Napkins are usually constructed from three layers of tissue paper. Only the top layer has a printed image. To peel apart the layers, start at any corner and separate the layers out. Pull them apart gently, taking care not to tear them.

TEARING AND CUTTING

Cut out an image using a small pair of scissors. If you prefer a frayed-edge look, tear out the image instead. First fold and crease along the desired border or edge with your fingertip. Then, supporting the tissue on both sides of the crease, tear little by little.

PASTING

Apply a thin layer of paste directly onto the object, rather than onto the tissue. Spread the paste over an area slightly larger than that of your design and gently lay the tissue image on top, smoothing carefully with your fingertips.

BRUSHING OUT

Use your brush to gently spread out the design. Take care, as wet tissue can easily tear.

WORKING ON A CURVED SURFACE

When working on a curved surface, such as an egg, you will need to accommodate all of the excess paper. Because the tissue is so fine, it will easily form pleats with careful brushing.

PASTING LARGER DESIGNS

If your design is fairly large, first wipe it gently to mop up any excess paste. Then lay a barely damp cloth over the surface and go over the image with a roller.

USING FOILS

Foil candy wrappers are a great resource and can be used to create a stunning effect in

découpage. Care must be taken when varnishing them, as solvents can dissolve the

colored surface. Use a water-based varnish or experiment with others. Some craft store

will stock a range of colored foils.

SMOOTHING FOIL

Lay your foil, color-side up, on a smooth surface and gently stroke across the foil until it is smooth. Don't apply excess pressure or you may stretch or tear the foil. For larger pieces of foil, you can use an iron to remove the creases.

TEARING FOIL

If you want your foil design to have rough edges, draw the shape onto the back of the foil leaving indented lines that you can then tear along. If you want a cleaner design, cut along the indented line instead. (See photo below left.)

APPLYING FOIL

Foil should be stuck down using glue. Take care when applying foil as it tears very easily and the surface color can be scratched. Use tweezers to position very small pieces of foil.

VARNISHING

For most of the projects in this book, four coats of varnish will be sufficient. However,

some items will need more protection from wear and tear, so allow at least six coats.

The Polka Dot Tray (see page 48) and the Chintz Chairs (see page 64) are examples of items that will need at least six coats. If you want to achieve a finely lacquered finish, you will need to sand between the layers of varnish. To achieve a smooth surface, rub harder over any areas where there are lumps or dust, but take great care not to rub through to your design. Wipe off any dust particles with a soft, barely damp cloth. Once dry, repeat the process, sanding between every second coat until you have the surface you are happy with.

Spray varnishes speed up the process. They are more expensive, but are better for irregular shapes such as eggs. Whether you use a water-based or oil-based matte, satin, or gloss varnish is mostly a matter of taste. Experiment on leftover print scraps. Polyurethane tends to darken prints and yellows slightly with age, which can be good if you want an antique effect.

APPLYING VARNISH

It is important to remember that many thin coats of varnish are better than a few thick ones.

Apply your varnish with a good-quality, flat, blunt-ended brush that will not shed hairs. Choose the size in relation to the object you are working on. Dip the tip of the brush into the varnish; don't overload it, as it will drip. Hold the brush at a forty-degree angle. Lightly drag the brush over the surface of your object. Work away from the center of the piece in the same direction as the wood grain, leaving a smooth, even coat. Then allow to dry thoroughly. Find a box large enough to cover your object to protect it from dust while it is drying.

VARNISHING AN EGG

If you don't want to use a spray varnish (see right), place reusable putty over the holes in the egg and insert a pushpin in the hole at each end. Use these to support and revolve the egg on a reel of tape as shown. Check that the egg clears the surface.

USING A LAZY SUSAN

A lazy Susan can come in handy when varnishing. You can turn an object without getting fingerprints on it. Cover it with a piece of foil or cling film to protect its surface while you work.

SPRAY VARNISHING

When using a spray varnish, it is useful to put your object on the lazy Susan, and place it inside a cardboard box. (Suspend eggs from the top of the box.) Wear a face mask to protect yourself from fumes. Slowly revolve the stand as you spray. The box will help stop the varnish particles from dispersing and will prevent dust from settling on your object.

TROUBLESHOOTING

Take care with each stage of a project and try not to rush any of the processes

involved. This way you will avoid making mistakes.

It is advisable to test the compatibility of your materials from the start. (Will the paper react to the glue? Does it stretch terribly? Does the varnish change its color or opacity?) Most mistakes are easily rectified, and if they can't be, then you can always add other smaller images over the top to camouflage them.

AIR BUBBLES

If an air bubble forms while you are gluing, gently peel back the print until you reach the bubble. Apply a little more glue, and using a spatula, ease the print back into place. If you discover the air bubble after the print is dry, use a sharp craft knife and cut along the nearest contour in your design to reach it. Lift the print carefully with the edge of your craft knife and apply some glue to the underside with a cocktail stick or pin. Then ease the print down, stroking out any air, and wiping away excess glue with a damp sponge. Allow it time to dry completely.

TEARS

Generally when a wet print tears, it doesn't happen in a straight line, but in a crooked line, usually with one side of the tear showing the white underside of the paper. This actually makes it easier to repair. Peel away the area involved and then repaste the torn side with the visible underside first. Apply minimal glue along this white edge, and place the other half of the tear on top, matching up the design. Lightly smooth it into place with a damp cloth, taking care not to move it out of alignment.

PEELING IMAGES

This tends to happen along the edges of an image where insufficient paste has been used. Take a craft knife and lift the peeling edge slightly, then force some glue underneath with a pin, brush, or cocktail stick. Press down firmly and maintain pressure for some time. Wipe away any excess glue. It may be necessary to place a weight (such as a telephone book) over the area to

ensure the edge stays down. Always place a piece of cloth over the image first, however, to protect it.

REMOVING A PRINT

If before varnishing you decide you don't like your design, don't despair. You can completely remove it. Use a warm, damp sponge or cotton swab to soften the glue at the edges of an image first. Then, using a fine, blunt edge, such as a spatula or palette knife, slide under the image and gently lift it little by little. Continue working in this way until you have completely removed the design. Any paper residue can be sanded off once the object is dry again.

FEATHERWEIGHT LAMPSHADE

Feathers add to the beauty of these stylishly simple lamps. Feathers can be scanned or

color copied, as can flowers, leaves, and shells (providing they are not too bulky).

However, take care not to scratch your scanner or the copier.

YOU WILL NEED

- Selection of attractive bird feathers

- Sheet of cardboard or paper 8½ x 11 in.

- Reusable putty

- Scissors

- Cutting surface

- Craft knife

- Lamp with plain fabric lampshade

- Paste (see page 19)

- Paintbrush

1 Tack the feathers down onto a piece of cardboard or paper with reusable putty. Make sure it is not visible. Scan the page or take it to your local copy store in a folder for a color copy.

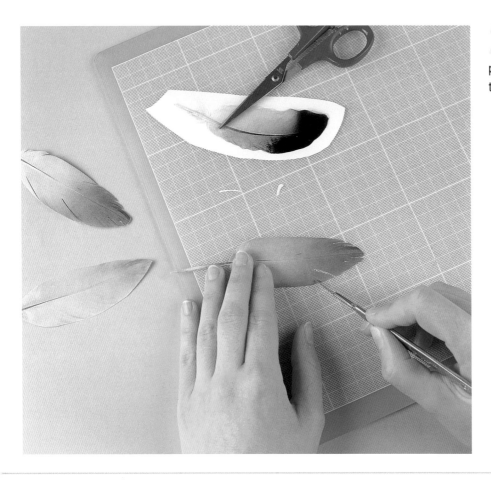

2 Cut out the general shape of each feather with scissors, then place on a cutting surface to cut out the fine detail using a craft knife.

ARTIST'S TIP

If you want to use the same feather, you can make multiple copies on your computer or copier.

3 Using reusable putty, tack your feathers around the lampshade at regular intervals. Walk away from the piece to view it from a distance. Make any necessary adjustments to achieve a harmonious design.

4 Paste each feather into position, taking care not to get any glue on the exposed areas of the shade. You may need to hold them down for a while until they adhere properly, as gluing onto a curved surface needs a little more care.

DESIGN VARIATION

Fairies are lovely to have on a lamp in a child's room. The light will illuminate them.

SWEET CHERRY COAT HANGERS

Simple wooden hangers are impressively transformed with a little bit of paint and some

cheerful images cut from wrapping paper. They are a nice addition to the room of a child

or teenager. This is a good project for newcomers to découpage.

YOU WILL NEED

- Wooden coat hanger
- Fine sandpaper
- Face mask
- Muslin cloth
- Water-based primer
- Paintbrushes
- Yellow emulsion paint
- Cherry wrapping paper
- Tweezer scissors
- Paste (see page 19)
- Sponge
- Water-based varnish

1 Sand off any existing varnish or paintwork from the coat hanger, remove the dust with a muslin cloth, and prime the wood. Once dry, apply the emulsion.

2 Before cutting out the découpage images, check whether any areas need thicker lines drawn on (see page 17), then cut out with small tweezer scissors.

3 Use a brush to apply paste to the back of the image, then position it on your fingertip and place it on the hanger. Wipe over the image with a slightly damp sponge, removing any excess paste, and allow to dry. Paste on further images until you are happy with the result.

4 Once dry, paint a layer of varnish over the hanger. Apply a second coat when the first is dry, and sand again when dry. Repeat the process with another two coats of varnish.

ARTIST'S TIP

It may help to put masking tape around the wire handle to avoid getting paint on it.

DESIGN VARIATION

For a teenager choose bright, fun colors and cut flowers from a sheet of wrapping paper. (See also the variations on page 27.)

PATCHWORK FRAME

This project uses a napkin with a pretty pink patchwork design. If you cannot find

something similar, you can create your own patches by cutting up squares of different

patterned paper and fitting them together. Alternatively, you could use fabric, but be sure

to use fine, tightly woven cotton.

YOU WILL NEED

- Paper napkin
- Wooden mirror frame
- Pencil and ruler
- Cutting surface and craft knife
- Water-based primer
- Paintbrushes
- Masking tape (optional)
- Hot pink and pastel pink emulsion paints
- Fine sandpaper
- Face mask
- Muslin cloth
- Paste (see page 19)
- Sponge spreader
- Cloth
- Roller
- Water-based varnish

1 Measure the napkin against your wooden frame and figure out what size border you will need to fit it. Then cut out the center of the napkin on your cutting surface, using a craft knife and ruler. Prime the wooden frame.

2 Once dry, use a pencil and ruler to mark where you want your inner and outer painted borders to be. For crisp lines, use masking tape to protect the areas you do not want painted. Color the inner border first, using the hot pink emulsion paint, making sure you don't forget the inner edge.

3 Paint the outer border, including the outside edge of the frame. When dry, give the paint a light sand, wipe away any dust with a muslin cloth, and apply a second coat to each border.

4 Remove the backing layers of tissue from the napkin. Apply paste to the appropriate area of the painted frame using a sponge spreader.

5 Carefully lay the print in position. Smooth out the tissue very gently with your fingers, being careful not to tear the paper. Lay a barely damp cloth over the print and roll across it with the roller. Cut a motif from the leftover napkin and place in each corner of the frame.

6 Once the tissue is dry, paint pastel pink stripes around both borders and leave to dry. Apply six coats of varnish, sanding between layers two and four.

LETTER RACK

Remind yourself of vacations on distant shores with this letter rack. Save postcards of

your favorite places or collect vintage cards. You don't have to use the original; you can

color copy or scan and print them, reducing them by 50 percent in size to fit your project.

YOU WILL NEED

- 🍃 **MDF blank letter rack**
- 🍃 **Fine sandpaper**
- 🍃 **Face mask**
- 🍃 **Muslin cloth**
- 🍃 **Water-based primer**
- 🍃 **Paintbrushes**
- 🍃 **Blue emulsion paint**
- 🍃 **Selection of vacation postcards**
- 🍃 **Scissors**
- 🍃 **Reusable putty**
- 🍃 **Pencil and ruler**
- 🍃 **Paste (see page 19)**
- 🍃 **Sponge**
- 🍃 **Water-based varnish**

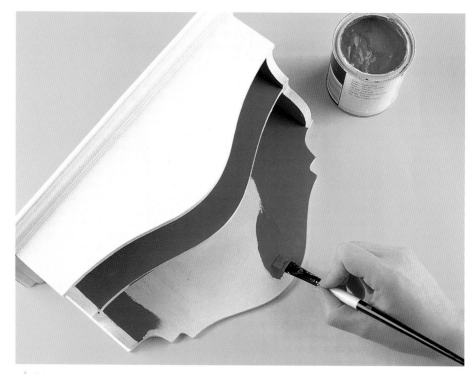

1 Lightly sand the blank letter rack and wipe off any dust with a muslin cloth. Prime the piece and leave to dry, then paint with two layers of blue emulsion. Sand between dry coats to get a really smooth finish.

2 Scan your postcards and reduce them 50 percent in size. Print out or color copy the images and cut them out using a pair of scissors.

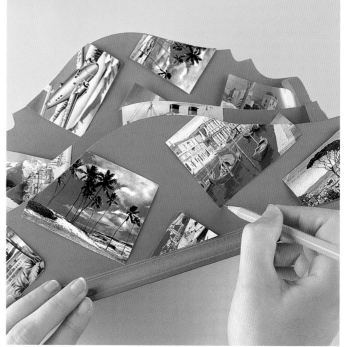

3 Using reusable putty, tack your prints to the letter rack at jaunty angles until you have achieved a pleasing arrangement. Mark out the positions using a sharp pencil and ruler.

34

4 Paste each postcard into place, carefully using a damp sponge to smooth out the images and remove excess glue. Allow to dry. Once the glue is dry, apply four layers of varnish, sanding after each second coat.

ARTIST'S TIP

Fifties postcards can be bought cheaply from swap meets and thrift stores.

DESIGN VARIATION

For a totally different effect, paint the letter rack in a pale color and use images of angels.

SCRUMPTIOUS PLATTER

Bronze powders give a metallic luster to this MDF blank plate. Chocolates shapes, cut from a sheet of wrapping paper, have been used for decoration, but you could also use images from advertisements in magazines. The surface on the plate has been finished with a spray gloss varnish. Take care when you clean this piece—use a damp cloth and don't put it in the dishwasher!

YOU WILL NEED

- **MDF blank plate**
- **Fine sandpaper**
- **Face mask**
- **Muslin cloth**
- **Water-based primer**
- **Paintbrushes**
- **Russet emulsion paint**
- **White school glue**
- **Bronze powders (fire copper and purple)**
- **Chocolate wrapping paper**
- **Scissors**
- **Colored pencil or felt-tip pen**
- **Pencil**
- **Paste (see page 19)**
- **Sponge**
- **Spray gloss varnish**

1 Lightly sand the MDF blank until smooth all over and wipe off any dust with a muslin cloth. Prime the plate and leave it to dry.

2 Apply two coats of emulsion, sanding between the dry layers.

3 Mix a thin solution of glue and fire copper bronze powder and lightly brush it around the border of the plate. Try to get an even distribution of the powder. Leave the plate to dry.

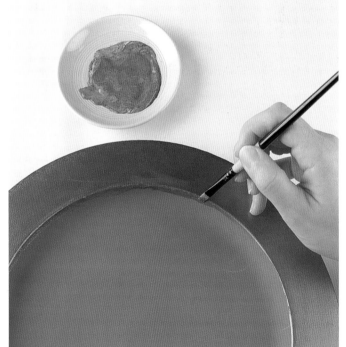

4 Make a second, denser, mixture of glue with bronze powder—this time purple. Use this to paint a thin edge around the rim of the plate and allow to dry.

5 Cut out the chocolates for your decoration. It is best to cut out more than you need, so that you can play around with the design until you achieve a pleasing result. Color the edges of your cutouts with a similar colored pencil or felt-tip pen (see page 17). Mark the final positions of the images with a sharp, hard pencil.

ARTIST'S TIP

If you can't find wrapping paper with chocolates, look at candy wrappers and boxes of chocolates.

6 Apply paste to the back of the prints one at a time and place them in their marked positions. Start with the most centrally positioned images, then radiate outward. Wipe off excess paste with a slightly damp sponge. Once completely dry, put on a face mask and spray-varnish the plate. Apply four coats, lightly sanding every second layer. Once the top is complete, don't forget to do the underside!

SEASHORE DRAWERS

It's not hard to transform a plain set of wooden drawers into a stylish piece of furniture.

This project uses a combination of images taken from wrapping paper, napkins, and

images from old books. The effect is to re-create a seaside scene.

YOU WILL NEED

- Small set of wooden drawers
- Fine sandpaper
- Face mask
- Muslin cloth
- Water-based primer
- Paintbrushes
- White and cream emulsion paints
- Shell wrapping paper
- Scissors
- Reusable putty
- Pencil
- Paste (see page 19)
- Spatula
- Sponge
- Seashore napkins
- Birds' egg color copies
- Flat decorators' varnish

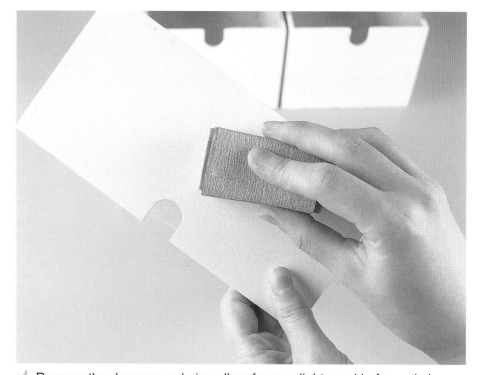

1 Remove the drawers and give all surfaces a light sand before priming, wiping away any sanding dust with a muslin cloth first. Once the primer is dry, paint the drawers with white emulsion and the cabinet with cream. Allow to dry. Apply a second layer and lightly sand until smooth.

2 Cut out the shells from the wrapping paper and tack to the base drawer with reusable putty. Mark their positions with a sharp pencil. Then, one by one, paste them into position, smoothing out the paper with a spatula and removing excess paste with a slightly damp sponge. Add a seagull cut from a seashore napkin.

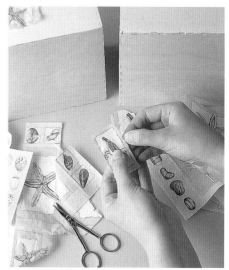

3 Tear out more images from the seashore napkins, and following the instructions on page 20, remove the backing tissue. Decide on an arrangement for the remaining drawers, then paste the appropriate areas and apply the tissue on top of the paste, one by one, smoothing them out carefully with a paintbrush.

4 Cut out the birds' egg color copies and paste into position to complement your arrangement.

5 Allow to dry, then coat the cabinet and drawers with flat decorators' varnish. This will give it a subtle finish. Apply four coats, lightly sanding between every second layer.

DESIGN VARIATION

This romantic set of drawers is painted in hot pink and purple. Flower wrapping paper surrounds it and Victorian scrap bunches of flowers decorate the drawers.

MAGAZINE RACK

The image on the front of this funky magazine rack has been cut out from leftover wallpaper. You can find similar images on the sides of store bags. Ask your wallpaper supplier to keep old sample books for you; they are a great resource for découpage.

YOU WILL NEED

- MDF blank or old magazine rack
- Fine sandpaper
- Face mask
- Decorators' filler
- Muslin cloth
- Water-based primer
- Paintbrushes
- Coral, hot pink, and yellow emulsion paints
- Two large flower prints
- Scissors
- Reusable putty
- Pencil
- Paste (see page 19)
- Spatula
- Sponge
- Cotton swabs
- Water-based varnish

1 Check that your MDF blank is smooth and that the joints are tight. If it is rough in places, sand it before priming. If there are gaps in the joints, fill them with decorators' filler, sand and wipe with muslin, then prime. Once the top is dry, don't forget to prime the base. Paint the inside of the rack first—starting with the inside base—using the coral emulsion. It helps to have a long-handled brush for this job (such as a radiator brush). Leave the paint to dry, then lightly sand before applying a second coat.

2 Once the inside paintwork is dry, you can start on the outside using the hot pink emulsion. Stand the rack on a piece of wood to enable you to paint all around the bottom edge. Apply two coats.

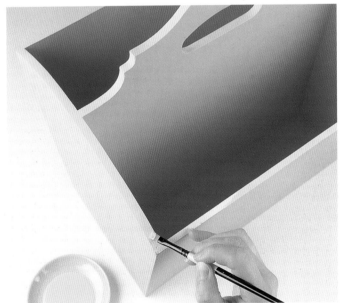

3 When the hot pink emulsion has dried completely, paint the edges of the magazine rack yellow. Apply two coats. Once all the painting is dry, lightly sand the rack for a smooth finish.

4 Cut out your design carefully and tack it in position with reusable putty so that you can view it from a distance. When you are sure of its position, carefully mark around it with a pencil.

5 Spread paste on to the back of the print and position it on the rack. Smooth out any wrinkles with a spatula, radiating out from the center. Wipe over with a slightly damp sponge to remove excess paste. Use a cotton swab to remove any paste trapped between the "valleys" of the petals. Repeat this process on the opposite side of the rack.

6 Apply varnish to the finished rack, first to the inside and then to the outside. Once dry, give a light sand and repeat for the second coat. Apply six coats of varnish, lightly sanding between every second coat.

ARTIST'S TIP

Cover the rack with a big box when you are waiting for each layer of varnish to dry to keep dust from settling on it.

EASTER EGGS

It is an old Easter tradition to blow eggs and decorate them to hang on a branch. These lovely eggs have been pasted with images cut from Easter napkins (their thin tissue easily molds around an egg's curved surface) and have been painted with pastel acrylic paints and hung from bright silk ribbons.

YOU WILL NEED

- Blown white eggs (see Artist's Tip)
- Easter paper napkins
- Scissors
- Paste (see page 19)
- Paintbrushes
- Pastel acrylic paints
- Eggcup
- String
- Large box
- Spray varnish (matte or gloss)
- Face mask
- Long dollmaker's or upholstery needle
- Thin silk ribbon

ARTIST'S TIP

Using a needle, scratch a small cross at each end of the egg. Gradually etch the shell until you have created a small hole in the center of the cross. Jab around inside the egg with a long needle to break up the yolk, then blow from the broadest end of the egg. Once the egg is empty, wash it in soapy water, making sure the inside of the egg is thoroughly washed. Rub the surface of the egg with vinegar.

1 Choose your images from the napkins. Cut or tear them out and peel off the backing tissue (see page 20). Decide on the position of your images, then spread paste over the appropriate area on the egg, holding it carefully with your thumb and index finger at either end of the egg. Place the image on the glue and smooth out with a paintbrush (see page 20).

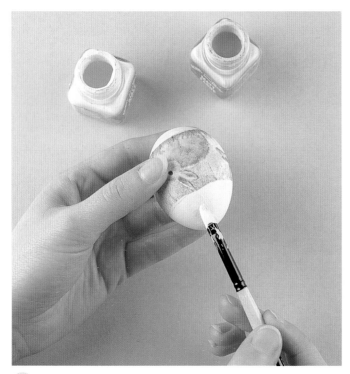

2 Once the glue is dry, you can paint the egg. Start by painting one end with a base color. Place the egg in an eggcup, the painted end on top, and leave it to dry. Repeat on the other end of the egg.

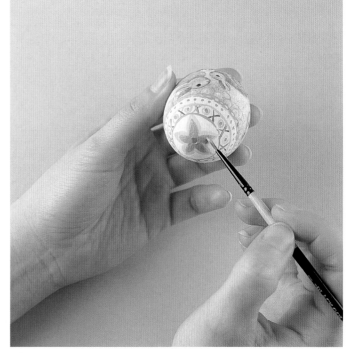

3 Using a fine brush, paint stripes of color around one end. Once dry, decorate these with patterns. Paint a flower around the end hole. Repeat at the opposite end.

4 When the body of the egg has been decorated, suspend it on a string in a large box and spray varnish in a well-ventilated room while wearing a face mask, or paint on varnish as described on page 22. When the varnish is dry, using the dollmaker's needle, thread up your silk ribbon and work it through from the bottom of the egg to the top. Make a loop at the top, and thread the needle back through the egg, tying the two ends of the ribbon in a knot at the bottom. Make sure that the knot is big enough not to slip into the egg.

DESIGN VARIATION

Blue and white is such a popular color combination to collect crockery in, so why not decorate some eggs to match? These motifs have all been cut from napkins.

POLKA DOT TRAY

Roses and polka dots are a very fashionable combination, and for this project I have found an easy alternative to painting dots. White self-adhesive dot stickers have been placed in position around the tray's sides. The roses are Victorian scraps (see pages 78–79 for details). Make sure to be generous with the layers of varnish for this project, as trays have to stand up to a lot of wear and tear.

YOU WILL NEED

- MDF blank tray
- Fine sandpaper
- Face mask
- Muslin cloth
- Water-based primer
- Paintbrushes
- Decorators' tape
- Blue, pink, and white emulsion paints
- White self-adhesive dot labels
- Pencil
- Small scissors
- Victorian rose scraps
- Paste (see page 19)
- Sponge
- Spatula
- Matte water-based varnish

1 Lightly sand the MDF blank and wipe the surface with a muslin cloth. Prime the top of the tray and allow it to dry. Once dry, turn it over and prime the sides and base.

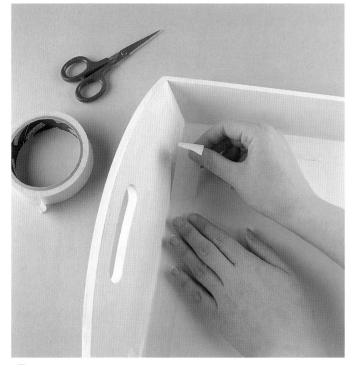

2 Line the inside edge of the base of the tray with decorators' tape.

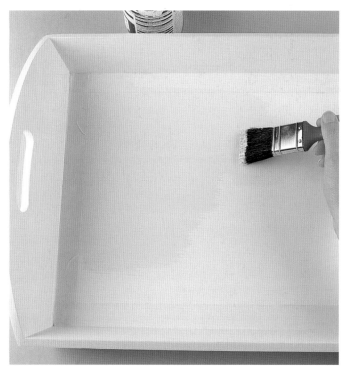

3 Paint the base of the tray blue with two coats of emulsion, sanding between layers. Once dry, remove the decorators' tape.

4 Now use decorators' tape to protect the blue paintwork, and paint the base border and the edges of the tray with pink emulsion. Once dry, turn the tray over and paint the underside—also in pink.

5 Using a thin, flat-ended paintbrush, paint white edging all around the rim of the tray. Allow this to dry, then sand before painting a second coat.

6 Figure out the positions of your polka dots, marking lightly in pencil. Place them at roughly regular intervals. Stick the dots into position, starting with the lowest row first.

ARTIST'S TIP

Use a pair of dividers to help figure out the intervals between the polka dots.

7 Use small scissors to neatly trim the edges of the Victorian rose scraps. Play around with the roses until you have achieved a pleasing pattern.

8 Lightly mark their positions with a sharp pencil, making sure the marks will not be visible once the roses have been pasted in place. Apply paste to the back of each rose and glue it into position on the base of the tray. Use a damp sponge to mop up any excess paste.

9 Smooth out the images with a spatula as you go. Once the paste has dried, use matte varnish to protect the tray. You will need plenty of coats to stand up to moisture and heat, so apply at least eight layers, sanding lightly between every second coat.

FAIRY BOX

An ordinary shoebox has been transformed to make a wonderful gift for a child.

Here, Victorian flower fairy scraps decorate the lid of the emulsion-painted box. Three-

dimensional sparkle and pearl paints have been applied to add a touch of magic.

YOU WILL NEED

- Shoebox
- Decorators' tape
- Water-based primer
- Paintbrushes
- Ruler and pencil
- Pink and blue emulsion paint
- Victorian flower fairy scraps
- Reusable putty
- Cutting surface
- Craft knife
- Paste (see page 19)
- Spatula
- Sponge
- Water-based varnish
- Pink and mauve three-dimensional pearl paint
- Three-dimensional glitter paint

1 If the corners of the shoebox aren't neatly and securely joined, tape over them—outside and in—with decorators' tape. Don't forget to do the corners of the lid too.

2 Prime the lid and the inside of the box. Allow to dry. Then prime the outside of the box.

3 With a ruler and pencil, mark out a border around the lid of the shoebox, and mask over with decorators' tape. Paint the center panel of the lid with two coats of blue emulsion, and allow to dry.

4 Remove the tape, then remask along the inside edges of the blue panel so that you can paint the border and the edge of the lid with a couple of coats of pink emulsion. While the lid is drying, you can paint the outside surfaces of the box with pink emulsion.

5 Select your flower fairy scraps and arrange them within the panel on the shoebox lid, marking out where they need to be cut and where they overlap each other. Then place on a cutting surface and cut to size using a craft knife (see page 17 for interlocking cutting).

6 Place the cutouts on the lid and mark their positions carefully with a pencil. Spread paste across the backs of the images, then press them into position and smooth over with a spatula. Wipe over with a barely damp sponge to remove any excess glue.

ARTIST'S TIP

Make sure that you spread glue right up to the edge of the images with a brush appropriate to the size of the print.

7 When the paste is dry, you can varnish the box. Apply four layers, allowing each layer to dry thoroughly before applying the next coat.

8 Once the varnish is completely dry, pipe around the edges of the panel and the box lid with little beads of three-dimensional pearl embossing paint. Alternate between pink and mauve. Do the inner edge first and leave to dry before applying the outer edge since it is easy to smudge the paint. Finally, add the scrollwork all around the edge of the shoebox lid in three-dimensional glitter paint, and leave to dry.

DESIGN VARIATION

This box has been decorated with roses and pearls. This would be a lovely box in which to keep bridal shoes.

SKY SCREEN

Screens can be useful for all sorts of reasons—for sectioning off part of a room, for privacy while changing, or for creating ambience. Using a purpose-made MDF blank screen, I devised a sky and seagull design using wallpaper and birds that I drew myself.

YOU WILL NEED

- MDF blank screen
- Fine sandpaper
- Face mask
- Muslin cloth
- Water-based primer
- Paintbrushes
- Blue emulsion paint
- 2 rolls of cloud wallpaper
- Pencil
- Scissors
- Paste (see page 19)
- Spatula
- Cloth
- Cutting surface and craft knife
- Color copies or printouts of seagulls (see pages 76–77)
- Reusable putty
- Matte spray varnish

1 Work with the screen in separate panels. Lightly sand the panels all over and wipe clean with a muslin cloth. Prime the edges of each screen panel and paint all visible edges with the blue emulsion. Don't bother to paint where the hinges will be fitted.

2 Unroll a section of wallpaper and lay, pattern-side down, on your work surface. Place a screen panel on top and draw around it with a pencil, allowing a ½ in. border. Cut this out.

3 Spread paste all over the wallpaper (if it is self-adhesive, follow the instructions). Fold the pasted paper in half to carry it. Position the bottom corners first, allowing for the overlap, and then unfold the paper out to the top of the screen. Smooth any bubbles from the center to the outside of the paper using a spatula. Wipe over with a damp cloth and leave to dry.

ARTIST'S TIP

Don't squeeze out too much of the paste, particularly at the edges, or the paper will lift off once dry.

4 Lay the panel facedown on a suitable surface for cutting. Using a craft knife, cut away all the excess paper, taking care not to shave the edges of the panel itself. Repeat steps 2 to 4 for both sides of all panels.

5 Photocopy or scan and print out the templates on pages 76–77. Cut them out. Use reusable putty to tack them onto the screen, playing around with them until you achieve a harmonious arrangement.

6 Carefully mark the seagulls' positions, then paste them onto the screen, smoothing them down with a spatula.

ARTIST'S TIP

You may also wish to use the seagulls to decorate a bathroom wall.

7 Apply several coats of matte spray varnish. Make sure you do this in a dust-free, well-ventilated room and wear a face mask.

8 Assemble the screen panels according to the manufacturer's instructions.

DESIGN VARIATION

Here I've used finely patterned origami paper to make and cut out clothes for this washing line. Make templates so that you can repeat the shapes. Use felt-tip pens to outline them.

FIREPLACE SCREEN

Birds and blossoms unite to create this design, reminiscent of a more traditional

découpage style. The lovely magnolias splay out across the screen while the birds perch

here and there among them. Both motifs have been cut from wrapping papers.

YOU WILL NEED

- MDF blank fireplace screen
- Fine sandpaper
- Face mask
- Muslin cloth
- Water-based primer
- Paintbrushes
- Cream and white emulsion paint
- Pencil and ruler
- Bird and magnolia wrapping paper
- Felt-tip pen
- Scissors
- Reusable putty
- Cutting surface and craft knife
- Pencil
- Paste (see page 19)
- Sponge
- Cloth
- Wood glue
- Water-based varnish

1 Sand the screen and wipe clean with a muslin cloth. Prime all elements of the fireplace screen separately and allow to dry. Paint the front and back of the screen with cream emulsion and allow to dry. Lightly sand before applying a second coat.

2 Once dry, carefully paint the edges of the screen and feet white. Allow to dry and repeat. Sand to ensure nice smooth edges.

3 Use a pencil and ruler to mark positions for the feet of the screen, making sure that they are equidistant from each edge.

4 Select the birds that you want to use from the wrapping paper, adding more detail to the images with a felt-tip pen, if necessary.

5 Cut out the magnolia flowers and individual birds carefully, following the instructions on pages 16–17.

6 Arrange the prints carefully until you achieve a satisfactory design. Mark out their positions with a sharp pencil, as well as any areas where they overlap. Cut the images so they will butt up against each other, following the instructions on page 17. This will give you a smoother, cleaner finish.

7 Paste the backs of the images and smooth them into their marked positions on the screen. Apply the largest prints first, smallest last.

8 Paste all elements of the design into position one by one, wiping each with a damp sponge to catch excess glue, then drying with a cloth.

9 Glue the feet into their positions using wood glue, making sure that they sit flat on the floor. Wipe off any excess glue with a damp sponge and allow the screen to dry in a standing position. Once the feet are dry, you may want to touch up the paintwork in that area.

10 Apply four coats of varnish with a broad, flat brush. Leave each layer to dry before giving it a light sand and applying the next coat.

ARTIST'S TIP

You may wish to have a reversible screen with an alternative scene on the back to suit the season.

CHINTZ CHAIRS

These painted wooden chairs add a fresh feminine touch to any room. Choose floral fabrics to make the cushioned seats. A scan can be taken of the same fabric and used to make the découpage cutouts for the back of the chair. If you don't have access to a scanner, take the fabric to your nearest copy store to have a color copy made.

YOU WILL NEED

- Painted wooden chair
- Large sheet of scrap paper
- Pencil
- Scissors
- Old wool blanket
- Embroidery needle and thread
- Floral cushion fabric
- Sewing machine and thread
- Tape
- Needle and thread
- Color copy of fabric design
- Paintbrushes
- Paste (see page 19)
- Spatula
- Sponge
- Water-based varnish

1 If possible, remove the seat from the chair to make a pattern of it for the cushion. If you cannot do this, place a large piece of paper over the seat to trace its outline in pencil and cut it out.

2 Use the pattern to cut out three pieces from an old wool blanket to make the cushion filler.

3 Sandwich the three filler layers together and blanket stitch around all the raw edges with embroidery thread. Sew crosses here and there in the center of the "cushion filler" to stabilize the layers.

5 Tack and machine sew a ½ in. hem along the back edge of each piece of fabric. Tack the two pieces together, still right sides facing, incorporating two lengths of 15 in. tape at each of the front corners of the cushion cover. Machine sew the sides and front of the cover, leaving the back open for inserting the blanket filler. Trim any excess tape.

4 Fold the seat fabric in half, right sides together. Using the seat pattern and allowing an extra ½ in. all around, carefully cut out two pieces of fabric.

6 Turn the cushion cover right-side out and press. Cut two pieces of tape 25 in. long. Fold each in half and stitch at each corner of the back opening.

7 Place the blanket pad inside the cushion cover, then overstitch neatly along the back opening (this can be undone for washing the cover at a later time).

8 Make color copies or scans from a piece of the cushion fabric. Choose an area that will make a good motif for the back of the chair and cut it out.

9 Arrange the image on the chair, making sure that it fits neatly. Paste into position, smoothing over with a spatula, and wipe with a barely damp sponge. Allow to dry.

10 The backs of chairs get a lot of wear, so it is important that you apply a number of layers of varnish following the instructions on page 22. When the varnish is dry, you can use the tapes to secure the cushion to the chair. Adapt the size of the tape accordingly.

ARTIST'S TIP

You could also choose an image from your wallpaper to coordinate with your chairs.

JEWELRY BOX

Candy foil wrappers come in wonderful, tempting colors and can be used to create

beautiful découpage. Care must be taken when varnishing foil, as some varnishes

may remove the surface color.

YOU WILL NEED

- MDF jewelry box blank
- Masking tape
- Fine sandpaper
- Face mask
- Muslin cloth
- Water-based primer
- Paintbrushes
- Dark blue emulsion
- Pencil and ruler
- Confectionery foils
- Scissors
- White school glue
- Water-based varnish

1 Cover the hinges of the box with masking tape. Sand all surfaces and wipe over with a muslin cloth. Prime the box, leaving each section to dry completely before moving on to the next. Paint the inside of the box and lid with blue emulsion and leave to dry.

2 Now paint the outside edges of the lid, the base of the box, and its feet blue. Paint a second coat once the first is dry.

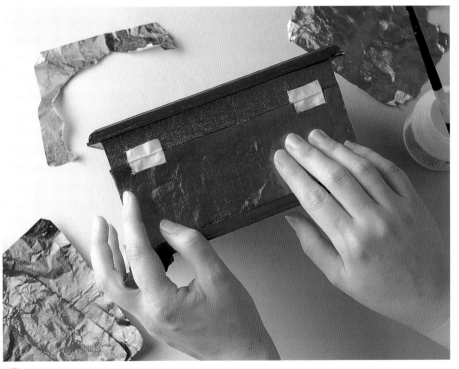

3 Measure all the dimensions of the box and cut a piece of foil to fit each side. Trim pieces to fit around any hinges. Glue into position.

5 Measure the top of the lid, and cut and paste a piece of foil to fit this. Repeat for inside the lid. Allow to dry.

4 Once all the sides are glued in place, allow the box to dry completely. Cut four strips of foil to fit the corner edges of the box and four to fit the corner edges of the lid.

6 Tear foils into shapes to make up your design for the lid (see page 21). Here I have torn petals, leaves, stems, and other pieces for a floral pattern.

7 Cut four strips of contrasting foil to make a border for the lid. Don't worry about having them all the same thickness—a little irregularity will add to the design.

8 Arrange the basic elements of the design and glue the pieces into position.

9 Gradually build up the design, adding the flower petals and finishing off with a circle in each corner.

10 Once all of the foil elements are completely dry, varnish the box, applying at least six layers and allowing each to dry before starting the next.

ARTIST'S TIP

Easter eggs are a great source of foils. Collect them and keep them pressed smooth in a big book.

CHRISTMAS BOX

Strong self-assembly storage boxes can be purchased. If you can't find one of these,

use a stylish ready-made one. Victorian scraps and Christmas images from a copyright-

free CD have been used to decorate this box. The original rope handles were replaced

with a more suitable cord to complete the luxurious feel of the piece. Use the box to

pack away your Christmas decorations or for transporting your presents.

YOU WILL NEED

- Self-assembly box (preferably)
- Water-based primer
- Paintbrushes
- Pencil and ruler
- Decorators' tape
- Green, red, and deep purple emulsion paints
- Cardboard
- Scissors
- Gold wrapping paper
- Paste (see page 19)
- Copyright-free images
- Victorian Christmas scraps
- Reusable putty
- Sponge
- Christmas border
- Thick gloss spray varnish
- Face mask
- Gold cord
- Three dimensional embossing paint

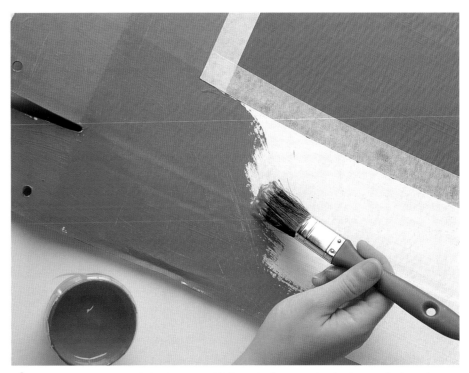

1 Prime the inside of the box and lid and allow to dry before priming the outsides. Using a pencil and ruler, mark out a 3 in. border around the top of the lid and a 2 in. border on each side of the box to give you a central panel on each visible surface. (The border widths can be adjusted according to the size of your box.) Mask off the borders with decorators' tape to paint the inside panel green. When dry, protect the green panel in the same way and paint the borders red.

2 Assemble the box and lid according to the manufacturer's instructions. Paint the inside of the box and lid with the purple emulsion. Allow to dry, then paint a second coat. Use the template on page 77 to draw and cut out a cardboard star. Use the template to cut stars from a sheet of gold wrapping paper. Paste them all over the interior of the box and lid at roughly regular intervals.

3 Choose the images you want to use from your copyright-free book or CD. Cut out the prints carefully and make a selection from your Victorian Christmas scraps. (An economic alternative is to use images cut out from Christmas wrapping paper.)

ARTIST'S TIP

You may prefer to use your favorite Christmas cards—this would be a great way to have them on display every Christmas.

4 Cut out the motifs for the panels on the sides of the box, allowing room for the holes that the cord handles will fit through. Taking each side one by one, tack the images to the green panel using reusable putty until you have the desired arrangement. Paste the images into position carefully, wiping each with a damp sponge to remove excess paste. Use little pictures where there are gaps and remember to leave room for the Christmas border.

5 Complete the design with a Christmas border, which finishes each panel with a clean edge. This one was enlarged 50 percent to fit the dimensions of the box. Position it and paste into place, wiping away excess paste with your sponge.

6 Choose the motifs for the lid of the box. Arrange within the green panel until you have achieved the desired result. Paste the images down and wipe clean any excess paste. Use the same or similar border, adjusted to the appropriate size, to complete the design.

7 Angels make a nice focus for the front panel of the box. Paste your chosen images according to your arrangement and surround them with a decorative border.

8 Once all the paste is dry, varnish the box—first the inside, then the outer surfaces. Use six to eight layers of thick, gloss spray varnish, sanding lightly between every second coat to achieve a smooth finish. Be sure to wear a face mask.

9 Thread your gold or silk cord through the holes in the side of the box, and cut the length accordingly—in this case it is 19 in. Tie a knot in both ends of the cord to ensure it does not slip out of the holes.

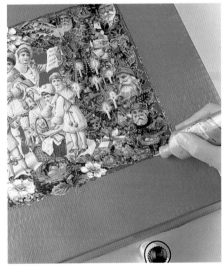

10 Use three-dimensional embossing paint to line the borders. It can be difficult doing long straight lines so make the lines slightly wiggly if you prefer.

TEMPLATES

Sky Screen (pages 56–59)
Set photocopier to 150 percent to copy images to correct size for project.

Christmas Box (pages 72–75)
Set photocopier to 150 percent to
copy image to correct size.

SUPPLIERS

Aaron Brothers Art & Framing
1270 S. Goodrich Blvd.
Commerce, CA 90022
(888) 532-9371
www.aaronbrothers.com

Artcity.com
1350 Kelton Ave., Ste. 308
Los Angeles, CA 90024
(866) Artcity
www.artcity.com

The Art Store
455 Fortune Blvd.
Milford, MA 01757
(888) 5-GO-ARTS
www.artstores.com

Art Supply Warehouse
5325 Departure Dr.
Raleigh, NC 27616
(800) 995-6778
www.aswexpress.com

Decoupage Supply Centre
26650 County Road 46A
Sorrento, FL 32776
(352) 383-3883
www.3d-decoupage.com

Dove Brushes & Tools
1849 Oakmont Avenue
Tarpon Springs, FL 34689
(800) 334-DOVE
www.dovebrushes.com

G & S Dye and Accessories Ltd.
250 Dundas St. W. Unit #8
Toronto, ON, M5T 2Z5
Canada
www.gsdye.com

Jo-Ann Fabric & Crafts
5555 Darrow Rd.
Hudson, OH 44236
(800) 525-4951
www.joann.com

Michaels
8000 Bent Branch Dr.
Irving, TX 75063
(800) Michaels
www.michaels.com

MisterArt.com
1800 Peachtree St. NW, Ste. 250
Atlanta, GA 30309
(800) 423-7382
www.misterart.com

Photosphere Ltd.
Dept. 8110—Ste. 413
250 H Street
Blaine, WA 98230
(800) 665-1496
www.photosphere.com

PictureQuest
8280 Greensboro Drive, Ste. 520
McLean, VA 22102
(800) 764-7427
www.picturequest.com

Suzi's Wood Crafts Plus, Inc.
29895 N. Stampede Rd.
Athol, ID 83801
(888) 941-0044
www.suziswoodcrafts.com

Target
(888) 304-4000
www.target.com

Texas Art Supply
2001 Montrose Boulevard
Houston, TX 77006
(800) 888-9278
www.texasart.com

Vintage Postcards
312 Feather Tree Drive
Clearwater, FL 33765
(727) 467-0555
www.vintagepostcards.com

Acknowledgments
The author would like to thank:

Frederick Warne & Co.—controls all rights in the *Flower Fairies* books on behalf of the estate of Cicely Mary Barker.

The Medici Society for permission to use their fairies wrapping paper by Margaret Tarrant.

Pete Andrew and **Kathryn Hughes** at **WAVE**, Buckfastleigh, and **James Gillmore**, **John**, and **Eric** for their help with the computer.

Cath Lucroft Mee for use of the fabric bunting shown on pages 2 and 64.

Andrew Gillmore and **Heidi Green** for looking after Bryany during the photography.

The author would also like to thank the following companies for supplying materials for use in this book: **Appli Craft**, **Dover Publications Inc. (31 East 2nd St, Mineola, NY 11501, http://store. doverpublications.com/)**, **Mamelok Press Ltd**, **OPITEC Hobbyfix**, **Scumble Goosie**, **The Stencil House**, and **William Robinson**.

INDEX

A

adhesives 12, 19
    to remove excess 19
air bubbles 23
antique effect 22

B

background 18
box: Christmas 72–5
    Fairy 52–5
    Jewelry 68–71
    rose and pearl 55
bronze powders 12
    to apply 15
    project using 36–8

C

chairs project 64–7
Chintz Chairs 64–7
Christmas Box 72–5
    star template for 77
coat hanger project 27–9
composition 18
copyright-free images 8
    project using 72–5
curves, to fit 17
cushions for Chintz Chairs
    65–6
cutting out 10, 11, 16
    fine lines 17
    interior areas 10, 16
    napkins 20

D

drawers: flower 41
    Seashore 39–41

E

Easter Eggs 45–7
edges: to cut 16
    to hide 13, 17
eggs: to apply image to 20
    to blow 46
    blue and white 47
    Easter 45–7
    to varnish 22

embossing 15
    see also three-
    dimensional paint
equipment 10–11

F

Fairy Box 52–5
Featherweight Lampshade
    24–6
felt-tip pens 13, 17
fine lines, to cut out 17
foils 8
    to apply 21
    project using 68–71
foreground elements 18
frame project 30–2

I

image(s): to apply to
    curved surface 20
    copyright-free 8,
    72, 74
    to cut out 16
    interlocking 17
    to mark position of 18
    to paste 19
    to prepare 16
    to remove 23
    to tear out 20
interior areas, to cut out
    10, 16

J

Jewelry Box 68–71

L

"lacquered" finish 6–7, 22
lampshade: fairy 26
    Featherweight 24–6
lazy Susan 10, 22
Letter Rack 33–5

M

Magazine Rack 42–4
masking 15, 49–50
materials 8
MDF blanks 7
    box 68–71
    fire screen 60–3
    letter rack 33–5
    magazine rack 42–4
    platter 36–8
    screen 56–9
    tray 48–51
metallic effect see bronze
    powders
mistakes, to rectify 23

N

napkins see paper napkins

O

origami paper 8
    project using 59

P

painting 14
paints 12–13
paper napkins 8
    projects using 30–2,
    45–7
    technique 20
pasting 19
Patchwork Frame 30–2
peeling, to rectify 23
photocopying 8, 25, 34, 67
platter project 36–8
Polka Dot Tray 48–51
postcards: project using
    33–5
priming 14

R

rack: Letter 33–5
    Magazine 42–4
rhythm, to create 18

S

sanding 14
    see also "lacquered"
    finish
scanning 8, 25, 34, 67
scissors 10, 11
screen: Fire 60–3
    Sky 56–9
    washing line 59
Scrumptious Platter 36–8
Seashore Drawers 39–41
Sky Screen 56–9
    templates for 76–7
stickers, self-adhesive 8
    project using 48–51
storage 8
Sweet Cherry Coat
    Hangers 27–9

T

tearing: foils 21
    napkins 20
tears, to repair 23
three-dimensional paint
    12, 15
    project using 52–5
tray project 48–51

V

varnishes 12
varnishing 22
Victorian scraps 7, 8
    projects using 41,
    48–51, 52–5, 72–5

W

wallpaper 8
    projects using 42–4,
    56–9
wrapping paper 8
    projects using 27–9,
    36–8, 39–41, 60–3